GENOCIDE

WHY DO WE LOOK AWAY

HOLOCAUST DIDN'T HAPPEN

GAZA IS NOT GENOCIDE

HOLOCAUST DENIAL

GENOCIDE DENIAL

ANTISEMITE

ARAB-HATER

INCLUDES ACCESS TO THE UN REPORT ON GAZA

DR. ABRAHAM KHOUREIS, PH.D.

THE APOSTLE OF COMPASSIONATE LEADERSHIP

Copyright Notice

Table of Contents

"To kill the innocent is to kill humanity itself; to look away is to let it die twice."

(Khoureis, 2025).

Open Eyes That Refuse to See

I stand before my audience often with a question that lingers longer than the lecture: *Why do human beings, who are capable of extraordinary compassion, so easily look the other way from the suffering of others?*

It is not a question born of curiosity alone. It is born of pain, of watching humanity fail its own moral test again and again. In my role as an adjunct professor of organizational behavior, and leadership expert and scholar I have spent years examining how individuals and groups respond to crises, injustices, and moral choices. I have seen how organizations build systems of belonging and inclusion and, at the same time, how they create structures of indifference. As a human rights and disability advocate, I have watched doors close in the faces of the most vulnerable, not because resources were absent, but because willpower was.

My deepest lens comes through the model I created, the *Compassionate Leadership Model and Pyramid*. This framework shows us that leadership begins at the base, in self-compassion, and rises level by level until it reaches its summit: serving others.

1

At the top level, we are called to embrace the dignity of *every* human being. But I caution my students, my clients, and myself: the higher you climb, the more you will encounter those who stand guard at the peak, leaders whose egos, interests, and fears drive them to block others from changing the status quo. These leaders do not embody compassion; they embody its opposite. And when genocide happens, it is often these very leaders who explain it away, justify it, or worse, enable it.

Why does the ordinary person look away? Why does the leader excuse the inexcusable?

Part of the answer can be found in human psychology. When we are confronted with suffering, especially suffering on a scale so massive it feels ungraspable, our first instinct is to protect ourselves. The human mind tricks us by telling us: *This is too much. This is not my fight. Someone else will step in.* On the level of individual behavior, this is the bystander effect, the same force that keeps a crowd silent while one person lies injured on the ground. On the level of nations and organizations, the same effect multiplies into a moral paralysis that allows genocides to proceed with the world as witness.

And here we are, in Gaza. A place where children's cries reverberate in real time through our screens, where satellites and drones give us images no generation before us has seen so clearly, where journalists on the ground show us hospitals turned to rubble and families starving. There is no excuse of ignorance. No claim that "we did not know." And yet, many turn their faces away. Leaders shake hands, sign contracts, and declare support for those who hold the weapons. Citizens scroll past images of lifeless bodies as if they were no more than background noise in the endless stream of content.

This is not simply a political failure. It is a failure of compassion at its highest level. It is the refusal to ascend the pyramid toward serving others. It is the choice to remain below, in comfort, convenience, and cowardice.

So, I return to my classroom and to my activism, and I ask again: *What is the cost of looking away?* For the victims, the cost is survival stolen, generations erased. For the bystanders, the cost is moral erosion, the slow death of empathy. For leaders, the cost is legitimacy lost, their names etched into history not as protectors of humanity but as accomplices to its betrayal.

We are reminded, then, that silence is not neutrality. Silence is action. To witness genocide and do nothing is to declare, without words, that the lives being destroyed are not worth the risk of our discomfort.

At the base of my Compassionate Leadership Pyramid is self-compassion, the ability to care for one's own dignity with the

purpose of serving the dignity of others. At its peak lies the duty to serve humanity. The space between these levels is where our choices reveal whether we will look away or whether we will see, and act.

THE COMPASSIONATE LEADERSHIP PYRAMID

SERVING
OTHERS

SOCIETY

COMMUNITY

ORGANIZATION

LOCAL ENVIRONMENT

NEXT OF KIN

SELF-COMPASSION

(Khoureis, 2021)

The Psychology of Turning Away

When I teach individuals and organizational behavior professional leadership workshops, I remind my audience that people are not simply rational actors. We are creatures of habit, fear, and fragile conscience. The same psychology that allows us to build communities of care can also allow us to retreat into silence when others suffer.

At the individual level, the bystander effect is one of the most studied phenomena. When a person collapses on a busy street, many will walk past, each one believing someone else will step forward. This is not because they are inherently cruel but because responsibility diffuses across the crowd. Inaction becomes normalized. The very presence of others reassures us that doing nothing is acceptable.

Now imagine that effect on the scale of nations. Leaders and citizens see genocide unfold, but each convinces themselves that intervention belongs to someone else: the United Nations, a neighboring state, the "international community." In this way, silence becomes collective. Nobody feels individually accountable, yet together they enable atrocity.

There is also the shield of distance. When tragedy strikes close to home, empathy is immediate. When it happens in another land, we rely on images, headlines, and narratives. The further the suffering feels from our daily lives, the easier it is to look away. For many, Gaza is a headline rather than a human reality. A photograph of rubble rather than a child buried beneath it. A statistic rather than a story.

But there is a deeper, more troubling mechanism: denial. To admit that genocide is occurring is to admit that humanity is failing. To admit failure is painful. So, people grasp at excuses, "It's a conflict," "Both sides are to blame," "They have been at it for generations," "It's too complex." Complexity becomes the language of avoidance. In truth, genocide is not complex. It is the systematic destruction of a people. It is the stripping away of humanity until lives are reduced to numbers.

For leaders, denial takes another form: calculation. Acknowledging genocide means acknowledging complicity, in weapons sales, in alliances, in silence. And so they shield themselves with political phrases: *We urge restraint. We support dialogue. We recognize the right to self-defense.* These words do not heal; they hide. They are carefully chosen to avoid naming the crime.

This is where compassion must intervene. My Compassionate Leadership Model and Pyramid teaches that the higher we climb, the more we are called to move beyond self-interest. Yet psychology shows us that most remain trapped at the lower levels, concerned with their own survival, their own comfort, their own reputations. It takes courage to rise, to serve others, to see suffering not as a threat to one's stability but as a call to moral responsibility.

In Gaza, the world sees children starving, hospitals without medicine, homes turned to dust. And still many turn away. This is not only a failure of politics but of psychology, the human instinct to protect the self at the expense of the other.

The challenge before us is not simply to expose atrocity but to dismantle the mechanisms of avoidance. To remind ourselves and our leaders that to look away is not neutral, it is an active choice. And every choice shapes the moral landscape of our time.

Leaders
and the Architecture of Complicity

When genocide unfolds, ordinary people often feel powerless. But leaders are not powerless. They have resources, alliances, and platforms that can alter the course of events. And yet, time and again, we see leaders either look away or lend their support, directly or indirectly, to the perpetrators. This is not accidental. It is structured. It is what I call the *architecture of complicity*.

In organizational behavior, we often study decision-making under pressure. Leaders frame choices not only by logic but by interests. They weigh costs and benefits, not always in moral terms, but in political and economic terms. When leaders support oppressive regimes, Israel for example in the Gaza case, it is rarely because they are blind. It is because they calculate.

One layer of this architecture is **geopolitical interest**. Arms contracts, trade agreements, and military alliances become bargaining chips. To acknowledge genocide in Gaza, for instance, would force certain governments to cut ties with their most lucrative weapons buyers. Leaders convince themselves that "national interest" outweighs moral responsibility. In doing so, they transform suffering into a line item in a ledger.

Another layer is **political survival**. Leaders are constantly watching their base, their donors, their voters. Taking a stand for justice can mean losing allies at home. It can mean being accused of weakness or betrayal. Many leaders fear the short-term backlash more than the long-term stain of silence. In classrooms, I remind my students, at my shops I remind my participants, and in my books, I remind my readers that leaders often behave less like visionaries and more like managers of their own reputation. They protect their image, not their conscience.

There is also the **language of framing**. Leaders who support atrocities rarely say so openly. Instead, they reframe the narrative: "security," "self-defense," "stability." These words mask the reality of indiscriminate bombing, starvation, and collective punishment. They give cover for violence by making it sound necessary, even responsible. Words become weapons as dangerous as bombs.

Finally, there is **collective shielding**. Leaders hide behind one another. If the United States remains silent, smaller nations follow suit. If Europe issues only cautious statements, others copy the tone. The result is a chorus of inaction, a harmony of excuses that protects everyone from standing out. I call this the organizational version of the bystander effect. Nations act like individuals in a crowd, waiting for someone else to step forward.

The Compassionate Leadership Model and Pyramid challenges this directly. At its peak is service to others, not service to interest, ego, or alliance. A compassionate leader would ask: *How do my actions protect the dignity of the vulnerable?* Yet most leaders stop climbing long before they reach this summit. Although traveling the levels of the pyramid depends on being mindful and self-aware, uncompassionate leaders linger at the environment of self-interest and self-preservation, unwilling to risk political or economic cost.

In Gaza, this architecture of complicity is visible. Leaders shake hands with those supplying the bombs. They veto resolutions calling for ceasefires. They praise "restraint" while hospitals run out of medicine. Each of these actions may appear as diplomacy, but in truth, they are bricks in the structure that enables genocide.

History remembers leaders not only for what they built but for what they allowed. Those who defend injustice in the name of security will be judged not as protectors but as accomplices. Silence and support are not opposites; they are twins in the same architecture.

So, the question becomes: what will it take to dismantle this structure? The answer begins not with politics but with conscience, leaders willing to climb higher on the pyramid, even when the peak is guarded by those who thrive on ego and fear.

Media, Silence, and Manufactured Consent

In every genocide, two forces move in parallel: the machinery of violence and the machinery of narrative. Bombs and bullets destroy lives; words and images distort truth. Together, they make atrocity possible. The public becomes conditioned not to see what is plainly visible, or worse, to see it and accept it as normal.

The media plays a decisive role. What is shown, what is hidden, and how events are described, these choices shape conscience. When the word *genocide* is avoided, when journalists frame Gaza as a "conflict" rather than a mass starvation and bombardment of civilians, the world learns to hesitate, to doubt, to pause compassion. Language numbs us.

Governments know this well. Leaders lean on media outlets to manufacture consent. They supply ready-made talking points, "Israel's right to defend itself," "security concerns," "anti-terror operations." These phrases appear on every screen, repeated until they feel factual. Meanwhile, the daily images of children in shrouds are sidelined as if grief itself were biased.

But behind the media framing stand the perpetrators. In Gaza, the primary hand is the Israeli government and its military apparatus, carrying out bombardments, starvation blockades, and systematic destruction of civilian life. These actions are not accidents of war; they are deliberate policies designed to break the spirit of a people. Israel calls it defense. In truth, it is collective punishment, the essence of genocide.

There is a deeper moral tragedy here: the perpetrators are a people whose identity was forged through the horror of their own genocide. The Holocaust, which annihilated six million Jews, remains one of humanity's darkest chapters. It should have been an eternal reminder that *never again* means never again for anyone, anywhere. Yet the state built in the shadow of Auschwitz now inflicts its own machinery of death on another people. To survive genocide and then commit one is a wound upon history, not only upon the victims but upon the survivors' own moral legacy.

This does not diminish the Holocaust; it makes it more urgent. The guilt lies not in memory, but in betrayal. The lesson of their suffering should have been universal, a beacon against future atrocities. Instead, it has been twisted into justification for the suffering of others.

And yet, Israel does not act alone. The United States supplies billions in weapons and shields Israel diplomatically, vetoing United Nations resolutions that call for ceasefires or accountability. European nations, while wringing their hands, continue to export arms and deliver the same diluted language of "balance" and "security." Arab regimes, desperate to secure their own survival, normalize relations and offer silence while their neighbors starve. Each one, by action or inaction, is a perpetrator in the architecture of complicity.

The media amplifies this betrayal. It repeats the language of power while muting the cries of the powerless. It interviews generals but rarely mothers. It frames bombs as strategy but seldom names the children buried beneath rubble. In this way, suffering is sanitized, made palatable for audiences who might otherwise revolt against the images before them.

As a human (all-human) rights advocate and as the creator of the *Compassionate Leadership Model and Pyramid*, I say plainly: when leaders, survivors, and institutions turn suffering into politics, they protect self-interest at the expense of others' humanity. They weaponize history instead of honoring it.

Gaza teaches us that genocide does not require ignorance anymore. It requires indifference. And indifference is manufactured, by governments, by media, and by those who choose silence over conscience.

The guilt will not fade. It will not be erased by treaties or press releases. History records who dropped bombs, who sold weapons, who vetoed justice, and who turned away. Just as the Holocaust is remembered, so too will Gaza be remembered, not only for the suffering inflicted, but for the silence of those who claimed "Never Again" and then made it conditional.

The Human Cost of Looking Away

When genocide unfolds, the most obvious victims are those whose lives are destroyed. But there is another victim often overlooked: humanity itself. Each time the world looks away, we lose a part of our collective conscience. Silence does not only harm the oppressed; it corrodes the soul of the bystander and stains the legacy of entire nations.

In Gaza, the human cost is written on the bodies of children. Starvation, once unthinkable in an age of global abundance, is now policy. Parents beg for flour while aid convoys are blocked. Hospitals run without fuel, surgeons operate by the light of mobile phones, and newborns gasp for air in broken incubators. This is not collateral damage. This is the deliberate strangulation of life.

For the survivors, the cost is not only physical but generational. Trauma seeps into memory, into childhoods marked by fear, into futures scarred by grief. A people who are dehumanized are forced to carry a wound that does not close. This is what genocide does: it erases not just the present, but the possibility of tomorrow.

But what of those who look away? What is the cost of silence? For ordinary citizens, the cost is the erosion of empathy. Each image scrolled past without pause, each headline rationalized away, dulls the moral nerve. We become accustomed to atrocity. The extraordinary becomes ordinary. That is how societies decay: not in sudden collapse, but in the slow death of compassion.

For leaders, the cost is far heavier. Every veto at the United Nations, every arms shipment approved, every excuse uttered in press conferences becomes part of the historical record. Just as we remember the leaders who appeased Hitler or who ignored Rwanda's cries, so too will we remember those who gave cover to the siege of Gaza. History has no mercy for enablers.

Then there are those whose silence is sharpened by irony: the Israeli state itself, born from the ashes of the Holocaust, now turning that memory into justification for crushing another people. This is the most tragic cost of all. To survive genocide and then inflict it is to betray one's own suffering, to desecrate the memory of one's dead. Instead of *never again*, it becomes *only for us, not for them.* That betrayal will reverberate across generations.

The *Compassionate Leadership Model and Pyramid* shows us that the peak of leadership is service to others. But Gaza reveals how many leaders remain trapped in self-interest and serving only themselves. The refusal to act is not neutral; it is a choice to protect comfort and alliances over conscience. The cost of that choice is measured in lives extinguished, but also in legacies destroyed.

As I continually remind my students and leaders clients, today, I remind you my dear readers:

To witness suffering and do nothing is to take sides.

To stay silent is to lend your voice to the oppressor.

To look away is to say, without words, that the lives of others are expendable.

That is the human cost of looking away, not only the death of others, but the slow death of our own humanity.

Breaking the Cycle of Indifference

Every generation has been tested by genocide. The world swore after the Holocaust that *never again* would human beings permit such destruction. And yet, Rwanda. Bosnia. Darfur. Gaza. The cycle continues, not because humanity lacks knowledge, but because humanity lacks courage.

Indifference is a learned behavior. It is passed down by governments that prioritize alliances over morality, by media that numbs conscience with euphemisms, by citizens who scroll past horror as though it were entertainment. To break the cycle, we must unlearn this reflex to look away.

The first step is **naming the crime**. Language matters. To call Gaza a "conflict" is to blur the truth. It is not a conflict between equals; it is the systematic destruction of a besieged population. Euphemisms give cover. Precision gives power. The world must have the moral clarity to say the word genocide when genocide is occurring.

The second step is **rejecting complicity**. Leaders must be held accountable for the weapons they supply, the vetoes they cast, and the silences they maintain. Citizens must see that democracy is not only about casting votes but about demanding conscience from those who govern. When leaders betray humanity, they do so in our name. Silence makes us co-signers of their crimes.

The third step is **learning from history honestly**. The Holocaust was not meant to teach that only Jews must be protected; it was meant to teach that no people should ever face extermination. To weaponize memory against others is to desecrate the very lesson history tried to give us. Those who survived genocide bear a special duty to ensure it never happens again, not only to them, but to anyone.

The fourth step is **rebuilding compassion as practice, not sentiment**. My *Compassionate Leadership Model and Pyramid* shows that compassion is not passive; it is active. It demands movement from self-interest to serving others. Leaders who stop at the lower levels, protecting their own interests, reputations, or alliances, fail the test. To serve others, especially the powerless, is the highest calling. This is what Gaza demands from us: the courage to act compassionately even when it costs us.

Finally, the cycle breaks only when **ordinary people refuse to normalize atrocity**. We cannot control governments alone, but we can control ourselves. Every time we pause to witness, to speak, to resist silence, we plant seeds of resistance against indifference. The smallest acts of solidarity matter, for they chip away at the culture of looking away.

Genocide thrives not only because perpetrators are ruthless and heartless, in which they are, but because bystanders are quiet. Breaking the cycle means shattering that quiet. It means reclaiming the conscience that has been dulled by politics, profit, and fear.

When I look at Gaza, I see unbearable suffering. But I also see a reminder, reflecting not only what is happening there, but who we are here. The question is no longer whether genocide exists in our time. The question is whether we will continue to live as if it does not concern us.

The cycle can be broken. But only if we dare to climb higher, as individuals, as leaders, as nations, toward the peak of compassionate leadership, where service to others becomes not an option, but a duty.

The Betrayal of "Never Again"

"Never again." Few phrases carry such weight in human history. Born from the ashes of the Holocaust, it was not just a declaration of grief but a pledge, that the organized extermination of a people would never be allowed to stain humanity again. It was supposed to be universal, a moral law above politics, a promise to all who suffer.

And yet, Gaza shows us how easily "never again" can be narrowed until it becomes "never again for us, but not for them." This is not merely hypocrisy; it is betrayal. A betrayal not only of Palestinians but of Jewish suffering itself.

The Holocaust was a crime against humanity on a scale that shattered conscience. Six million Jews murdered, alongside millions of others deemed undesirable. Survivors carried the memory in their bodies, their scars a living testimony. That memory should have been a guiding light, teaching that dehumanization anywhere is a threat to humanity everywhere.

Instead, in the state of Israel, forged in the shadow of that genocide, memory has been weaponized. The trauma of persecution has been twisted into justification for domination. The very suffering that should have taught empathy has, in the hands of the powerful, been converted into a shield for cruelty.

This betrayal is profound. To survive genocide and then impose blockade, starvation, bombardment, and collective punishment on another people is to desecrate the meaning of survival. It is to dishonor the dead by repeating, in new form, the crime that was supposed to end with them.

But we must be clear: this is not about Jews as a people. It is about the Israeli state and those who wield power within it. Many Jewish voices, in Israel and across the world, have cried out in opposition, refusing to let "never again" be corrupted. They understand that the true legacy of their suffering is solidarity with the oppressed, not silence before oppression. They remind us that "never again" must mean never again for anyone.

As a human rights advocate and as the creator of the *Compassionate Leadership Model and Pyramid*, I see in this betrayal the clearest sign of failed leadership. At the peak of the pyramid lies service to others. Yet here, leaders stand guard at the top, defending their own survival while crushing those below. Instead of rising above history, they repeat it in another form.

The betrayal of "never again" will haunt us if we let it pass unchallenged. For the Holocaust taught us not only what was done to Jews, but what humanity is capable of when silence prevails. To allow Gaza to become another chapter of extermination is to prove that the promise of "never again" was never universal at all.

The question is not whether the world remembers the Holocaust. It is whether the world has learned from it. Gaza is the test. And so far, humanity is failing.

The Silence of Allies

Genocide never happens in isolation. It requires perpetrators, but it also requires allies, those who supply, those who shield, those who look the other way. In Gaza, the silence of allies has been as deadly as the bombs themselves.

The United States stands at the center of this silence. Billions of dollars in military aid flow to Israel year after year, regardless of how many schools are bombed or how many children starve. American leaders speak of "shared values" while sending weapons that flatten homes. At the United Nations, U.S. vetoes block resolutions that would call for ceasefires or investigations. With each veto, the world is told: Palestinian lives do not count the same.

Europe, too, wears the mask of conscience while feeding the fire. Leaders issue statements of "concern" even as their countries approve arms sales. They organize conferences on human rights while ignoring the hospitals reduced to rubble. In the streets of London, Paris, and Berlin, citizens march for Gaza, but their governments side with power, not with justice.

Then there are the Arab and Muslim regimes. Their betrayal cuts deepest. While their people flood the streets demanding solidarity with Gaza, their rulers normalize relations with Israel, sign trade deals, and shake hands in public. In private, they fear the same fate as Palestinians, dispossession, rebellion, collapse, so they secure their thrones by appeasing the very forces crushing Gaza. Their silence is not born of ignorance; it is born of greed.

This silence is not passive. It is engineered. It is maintained through weapons contracts, diplomatic calculations, and the careful crafting of language. Every statement that calls for "restraint on both sides" is a denial of reality, that one side drops bombs and the other digs children from rubble. This false equivalence is complicity disguised as balance.

The *Compassionate Leadership Model and Pyramid* teaches that true leadership means rising above self-interest to serve humanity. But the silence of allies shows leaders trapped at the lowest levels, guarding alliances, profits, and reputations. They are not neutral; they are participants. Their silence is an endorsement stamped with the seal of diplomacy.

History has already recorded this pattern. During

the Rwandan genocide, Western powers debated the meaning of the word "genocide" while hundreds of thousands were slaughtered. In Bosnia, Srebrenica fell while peacekeepers stood aside. In Gaza, the cycle repeats: leaders issue statements, hold summits, and do nothing.

The silence of allies does more than protect perpetrators. It teaches the world that some lives are negotiable. That justice can be postponed. That dignity is conditional. And once humanity accepts that, no one is safe.

In the end, Gaza will not only be remembered for the bombs that fell, but for the silence that followed. The allies who chose politics over conscience will find their names written not among the defenders of humanity, but among its betrayers.

The Role of Ordinary Citizens

It is tempting to believe that genocide is the work of governments and armies alone. But history teaches us otherwise. Genocide requires more than weapons; it requires permission. That permission is granted not only by leaders but by ordinary citizens who choose silence, denial, or indifference.

When I teach organizational behavior, I remind my students that cultures are not built by laws alone, they are built by habits. In societies where people learn to look away from injustice, leaders are emboldened to deepen cruelty. In societies where citizens refuse silence, even the most powerful must hesitate. The fate of the oppressed often hinges on what ordinary people accept as normal.

Today, ordinary citizens across the world scroll past images of Gaza without pause. The sight of children pulled from rubble, of mothers holding lifeless babies, has become part of the endless stream of content. Horror competes with entertainment, and in the competition, horror loses. To witness without reacting is to normalize atrocity.

Some say, "It is complicated," and use that phrase to excuse inaction. But complexity is not an excuse for silence. No one needs a Ph.D. to know that starving children is wrong, that bombing hospitals is criminal, that erasing an entire people is genocide. Complexity is the language of those who would rather protect comfort than confront conscience.

Others hide behind distance. Gaza is far away, they say. But genocide knows no borders. To ignore it is to strengthen the machinery of indifference, which one day may turn inward. When we accept the suffering of others, we prepare the ground for our own suffering to be ignored.

Still others remain silent out of fear, fear of losing friends, jobs, or status by speaking unpopular truths. But silence is not safety. Silence is surrender. It allows violence to flourish unchecked.

Ordinary citizens are not powerless. They can raise voices, protest, boycott, write, and refuse to be numbed by the narratives of power. In Rwanda, it was ordinary radio listeners who became either enablers or resistors. In Nazi Germany, neighbors chose to denounce Jews or to hide them. In Gaza, the same question faces us now: will we stand with the victims or with the silence that kills them?

The *Compassionate Leadership Model and Pyramid* does not apply only to presidents and generals; it applies to each of us. At its base is self-compassion, the ability to preserve one's dignity. But as we climb, we are called to extend compassion outward: to families, to communities, to strangers, and finally to humanity itself. Every citizen has the choice to ascend or remain below.

The truth is simple: genocide cannot survive without bystanders. Perpetrators rely on silence as much as on weapons. Every time an ordinary person looks away, the machinery tightens. Every time someone speaks, resists, or refuses indifference, the machinery falters.

In Gaza, as in every genocide before it, the question for ordinary citizens is not whether they have power. It is whether they will use it.

Gaza's Legacy for Humanity

Every genocide leaves behind two legacies: the suffering of its victims and the testimony of its witnesses. The victims carry wounds, both visible and unseen, that pass down through generations. The witnesses carry shame or honor, depending on whether they chose silence or resistance. Together, these legacies shape how history remembers not only the genocide but the humanity that allowed it.

Gaza will not fade quietly into the margins of history. It is too well-documented, too visible, too undeniable. The rubble, the mass graves, the starving children, the blocked aid convoys, all of it is preserved in real time by cameras, satellites, journalists, and the voices of survivors. Future generations will not ask whether it happened. They will ask why so many watched and did nothing.

In Warsaw, we remember the ghetto not only for Jewish resistance but for the cruelty of those who walled in families to die. In Rwanda, we remember the hundreds of thousands slaughtered in a hundred days and the shame of the world that looked away. In Bosnia, Srebrenica stands as a monument to what happens when "peacekeepers" choose neutrality over protection. Gaza will stand beside them in the ledger of humanity's failures, unless we change course now.

But Gaza is not only tragedy; it is testimony. It reveals the nature of power in our age. It shows how governments calculate lives against profits, how media manufactures silence, how leaders betray memory, and how citizens numb themselves into complicity. Gaza is a mirror, forcing us to see not only the destruction of Palestinians but the decay of our own conscience.

Yet within Gaza's suffering there is another legacy: resilience. Despite bombs, starvation, and displacement, Palestinians endure. They sing, they write, they tell their stories. They bury their dead and still demand dignity for the living. This resilience is a rebuke to the world. It says: *you may look away, but we remain here. This is our land. As the Crusaders left before you, so you shall.*

The *Compassionate Leadership Model and Pyramid* teaches that leadership at its peak is not about survival of the powerful but service to the powerless. Gaza exposes how far the world is from this summit. But it also calls us higher. It challenges leaders, citizens, and

33

nations to rise above fear and calculation, to rediscover the duty of compassion.

Gaza's legacy for humanity is not yet sealed. It will be written not only by what happens there, but by what we choose to do here. If we remain silent, Gaza will join the long list of places where humanity failed. If we act, Gaza can become the place where the cycle finally broke, where "never again" regained its true meaning.

History waits for our answer. Gaza will be remembered. The only question is: will it be remembered as the wound that proved humanity's indifference, or as the turning point that restored its conscience?

Gaza's Children Speak

If history is honest, it will say that the children of Gaza carried the heaviest burden. They were not soldiers. They were not politicians. They did not sign treaties or launch rockets. They were children, and yet they became the first targets, the first to starve, the first to die.

The world often speaks about Gaza in numbers. Casualty counts, statistics of displacement, charts of aid deliveries. But behind each number was a child with a name, a face, a laugh, a dream. A child who wanted to play football, to draw pictures, to hold their mother's hand. Genocide reduces them to figures; conscience restores them to human beings.

When we hear their voices, even faintly, they speak not of politics but of life itself.

"I am hungry."
"I want to go home."
"Where is my brother?"
"Why are the Jews bombing us,
after we gave them shelter?"

These questions need no policy analysis. They require only compassion. Yet the world answered with silence.

To survive genocide is to carry trauma that lasts a lifetime. But for many of Gaza's children, there was no lifetime to carry. Their voices were cut off mid-sentence. Their dreams ended beneath rubble. Their drawings left unfinished. Their classrooms turned to dust.

The children of Gaza speak still, not with words but with memory. Their images haunt our screens, their faces press against our conscience. They ask us, silently now, *"Why did you look away?*

The *Compassionate Leadership Model and Pyramid* was built on the principle that leadership finds its highest expression in service to others. If there is any doubt what that means, listen to Gaza's children. To serve others is to protect them when they are powerless, to safeguard their right to live, to ensure their voices are not lost. To fail them is to betray the very meaning of humanity.

When the children of Gaza speak, they do not only tell their own story. They testify about us. About whether we chose silence or action, complicity or compassion. Their legacy will not fade, because it is written into the conscience of all who witnessed.

The children speak still. The only question is whether we will listen.

Why People Become Ruthless

Ruthlessness does not arrive fully formed. It grows in the shadow of ordinary decisions and quiet compromises. It is a moral weather system that develops over years: small acts of cruelty condense into policy, policies harden into orders, and orders, once obediently followed, become the architecture of annihilation. Understanding how this happens is not an academic exercise. It is the only way to prevent repetition.

Begin with language. Words matter. The first step on the road to cruelty is to rename a people. Labels remove human complexity. Where once there were parents, teachers, shopkeepers, and children, there soon are only categories: enemy, terrorist, expendable, shield. Dehumanization is the oldest tactic of mass violence. It is the tool that permits otherwise decent people to look away. When a human being is reduced to an object, violence becomes administratively easier and morally cheaper.

Next, consider authority and obedience. Social psychology has taught us painful truths. Ordinary people follow orders when the cost of disobedience is high and when institutions reward conformity. A soldier who refuses an order faces ostracism, court-martial, or worse. A civil servant who refuses to compile lists or sign directives risks unemployment. Obedience is not just a personality trait. It is a system property that can be enabled or disabled. Empires and states know this and exploit it. They cultivate hierarchies in which the moral question is outsourced up the chain. "I was only following orders" is not an excuse but an explanation of how systems manufacture culpability.

Third, ideology and moral disengagement provide the script. When cruelty is reframed as necessity, patriotism, or survival, conscience is rerouted. The language of security rearranges moral priorities: sacrifice becomes duty, and victims become collateral. Religious or ideological narratives can sanctify acts that violate any basic sense of human decency. The mind does not snap into brutality; it acquires a justification that makes brutality seem not only permissible but righteous.

Fourth, the bureaucratic mind sustains cruelty. Genocide is often not a flame but a factory. Paperwork, checklists, reports, memos, and budgets create plausible layers of normality. Bureaucracy disperses responsibility. When many hands touch a file, each hand can claim it merely processed a piece of paper. Yet each signature, each data entry, each logistic decision builds the scaffolding that allows mass harm to happen. We underestimate the moral power of forms.

Fifth, fear and scarcity corrode empathy. Leadership that governs through fear teaches citizens to put survival ahead of compassion. When a nation is convinced that resources are zero-sum, when security rhetoric promises safety only through exclusion, popular appetite for cruelty can rise. This is not inevitable. It is conditioned by political choices, by manipulative media, and by leaders who choose to stoke scarcity rather than to expand solidarity.

Finally, silence and complicity complete the circle. Silence is not neutral. It is a choice that benefits perpetrators. When journalists are intimidated, when courts are circumvented, when foreign governments choose commerce over conscience, silence solidifies into protection. Complicity often takes the form of distraction: humanitarian aid becomes an afterthought while geopolitical games continue; investigative bodies are starved for funds while rhetorical condemnations multiply.

To explain ruthlessness is not to excuse it. Explanation is the prelude to prevention. Each mechanism I have named is reversible. Dehumanizing language can be resisted by naming the human person. Obedience can be countered by institutional protections for dissent and by training that elevates conscience. Bureaucratic processes can be scrutinized, audited, and rendered transparent. Scarcity can be reframed by policies that expand support rather than scapegoating neighbors. Silence can be pierced by independent press, by scholarly investigation, and by an engaged global civil society.

History offers hard lessons. In the years before other genocides, many citizens reported feeling they were doing nothing unusual. They woke, they had breakfast, they wrote letters, they continued their work. That ordinariness is the danger. The banality of cruelty is its stealth. The antidote is to make ordinary acts courageous. When an office clerk refuses to sign a death list, when a pilot refuses a flight, when a minister publicly resigns rather than approve a policy of annihilation, those acts matter. They are the seeds of resistance.

Ruthlessness is therefore both a personal failure and a structural one. It demands a response on both levels.

We must teach moral courage and design systems that reward it. We must tighten the architecture of law so that no bureaucratic form shields atrocity. And we must cultivate a culture that keeps human faces at the center of political debate, even when faces are inconvenient for those in power.

If there is a single moral truth here let it be this: cruelty grows where we permit it to grow. We feed it in silence, we nurture it with euphemisms, and we water it with fear. Remove the fertilizer, name the harm, make accountability inevitable, and the soil will no longer support such growth. That is not utopia. It is practice. It is the work that safe, decent societies must do if they truly say never again.

Pursuing Accountability While Hunting the Perpetrators

There is a hunger inside victims and their families that law alone cannot fill. They want justice, public recognition, reparation, and a record that says, in an unmistakable voice, this happened, and these people are responsible. There is also a danger: when justified rage turns to private vengeance, the moral order collapses and the line between hero and criminal blurs. The only path that preserves the moral authority of victims is to insist on accountability that is disciplined, transparent, and lawful.

Justice begins with truth. The first imperative is documentation. Evidence is the instrument that turns accusation into conviction. Medical records, chain-of-custody for physical evidence, satellite imagery, open-source videos with verified metadata, survivor testimony recorded with forensic standards, and properly catalogued burials are not optional. They are the bones of any later legal process. Invest in teams trained in forensic methodology. Protect databases. Keep original files secure. The moral refusal to document is the moral equivalent of surrendering evidence to the void.

Independent investigation is the second pillar. Bodies with a clear mandate and operational independence must be able to enter, examine, and report. This is the domain of commissions of inquiry, hybrid investigative units composed of local and international experts, and UN fact-finding missions. Their legitimacy rests on impartiality. They must be insulated from political interference, funded adequately, and empowered to gather testimony without fear for witnesses' lives.

Third, use the law that exists. The International Criminal Court, despite its limits, is a tool. National courts with universal jurisdiction are tools. Regional human rights courts are tools. Civil litigation in foreign jurisdictions is a tool. Each venue serves a different purpose. Criminal courts aim to punish those most responsible. Civil suits can offer victims remedies and reveal networks of complicity. Sanctions and asset forfeiture hit the economic structures that enable atrocity. Together they make a web of accountability that is harder to evade.

Fourth, protect witnesses. The truth is fragile until it is made public. Witness protection programs, secure testimony channels, asylum options for whistleblowers, and psychological support for survivors are moral necessities. Courage without protection is dangerous courage. The international community must be ready to offer safe haven to those who bring forward the truth.

Fifth, pursue institutional reform. Perpetrators do not act alone. They act within institutions that either enable or block them. Police, militaries, intelligence services, and civil administrations must be audited. Command responsibility must be enforced. Leaders who issued immoral directives must be removed from power, and structural incentives that reward obedience over conscience must be restructured.

Sixth, use targeted financial measures. Sanctions are not simply political punishment. They can be surgical pressures placed on individuals, banks, trading partners, and logistics networks that support atrocities. Asset tracing and freezes, coordinated across jurisdictions, choke the resources that buy weapons, finance propaganda, and protect perpetrators. The goal is to isolate, not to punish entire populations.

Seventh, create public memory. Trials matter because they are public acts. The record preserved in court transcripts, forensic reports, and museum exhibits ensures that the truth is visible for future generations. Education systems must take responsibility. School curricula should not whitewash history. Monuments should remember victims, not glorify perpetrators. Memory is a civic resource that immunizes societies against repetition.

Eighth, mobilize civil society. NGOs, independent media, humanitarian groups, and diaspora communities play an indispensable role. They fund investigations, keep stories alive, provide legal assistance, and pressure governments to act. A vibrant civil society is often the first line of defense against forgetting.

Ninth, coordinate diplomatic pressure. Governments that value human dignity must translate that value into consistent policy. Diplomatic isolation of perpetrators, conditional aid, and public denunciations matter when they are backed by clear actions. Diplomacy cannot be merely rhetorical. It must be organized around enforceable consequences.

Tenth, do not neglect reparations. Justice includes restoration. Financial compensation, land restitution where possible, public apologies, and institutional guarantees against future abuse have restorative power. They acknowledge harm and provide victims with tangible recognition.

These mechanisms require time and stubbornness. Justice is not a theatrical moment. It is a long, difficult process that asks institutions to keep faith with victims when it is inconvenient and politically costly. Yet history shows that durable justice, even if slow, prevents cycles of revenge and builds the ground for reconciliation.

There are models to study. The Nuremberg Trials created a catalogue of crimes that remains a reference. South Africa's Truth and Reconciliation Commission combined public testimony with conditional amnesty to open a civic dialogue. The International Criminal Tribunal for Rwanda, established legal definitions and preserved records. Each model taught different lessons about prosecution, memory, and healing. We must learn from all of them and adapt.

Finally, the ethics of pursuit must be constant.

We must never imitate the cruelty we condemn. We must not weaponize suffering for political gain. We must not permit a politics of humiliation. Justice pursued through law preserves human dignity and reaffirms it. That is the moral victory. That is the lasting testimony.

A Letter to Leaders
Your Name in History

Power is a temporal gift. History is a long ledger. The two do not always align. Some leaders, intoxicated by short-term gain or gripped by a warped vision of destiny, imagine themselves exempt from moral accounts. They are not. The ledger of history is patient. It keeps full records.

If you preside over policy that denies food, blocks medicine, flattens neighborhoods, and kills children, understand this: the machinery of denial will not erase what you have done. Law will follow when it can. Memory will follow even when law cannot. Your speeches will be archived, your orders will be read, and your name will be associated with what you chose to do.

Consider those who came before you who believed in the permanence of their designs. They built monuments to permanence and found instead that their names became shorthand for atrocity.

They imagined loyalty and found condemnation. They believed they could secure a place in an honorable lineage and were instead placed in the catalogue of shame.

If you choose the path of denial and destruction, history will not be silent. Monuments may outlast you for a while. International politics may defer to expedience. But the record will be kept. Scholars will reconstruct the chronology, auditors will follow the money, journalists will unearth the memos, and the names of victims will be read aloud.

To those who now hold power I say this bluntly: you will stand before the judgment not of a single tribunal but of countless witnesses across time. Your deeds will be taught in classrooms. They will be spoken of in other nations. They will be read by descendants who ask why their grandparents were not protected, why the world failed them.

Yet there is still a human opening. Repentance is not a sign of weakness. It is the final exercise of moral leadership. Lay down tools of destruction. Invite independent inquiries. Offer reparations and public apologies that are genuine, not theatrical. Dismantle systems of impunity and show your people a different model of courage: the courage to confess error, repair harm, and build institutions that safeguard human dignity.

If you refuse, make no mistake: your name will not be spared. You will join the company of those history instructs as warnings. That is not hyperbole. It is what memory does. It arranges stories so that future citizens can learn the cost of cruelty. Choose your legacy with care. Power is fleeting. Conscience is not. The world will remember.

MY Final Thoughts
A Witness with Action

We live in an age where no one can truthfully say, *"We did not know."* Gaza is broadcast in real time. The images are unfiltered. The cries are unmuted. The truth is visible to all who dare to see it. The question is not whether we are witnesses, the question is whether we will remain bystanders.

History does not absolve silence. Silence is not neutrality; it is complicity. To witness genocide and do nothing is to declare, without words, that the victims do not matter. That their lives are expendable. That justice can wait.

The lesson of every genocide, from Auschwitz to Kigali to Srebrenica, was supposed to be *never again.* Yet each time, the world narrows the meaning of those words until they protect some but not others. Gaza exposes this betrayal. It shows us that "never again" is meaningless unless it is universal.

As a professor of organizational behavior, as a human rights advocate, and as the creator of the *Compassionate Leadership Model and Pyramid*, I say this plainly: leadership at its highest level is service to others. To refuse this duty is to descend into the architecture of complicity, where ego and interest replace humanity. The leaders who stood by in silence, who sent weapons, who vetoed justice, did not serve humanity. They served themselves. And I promise their names will be remembered not as protectors of peace, but as accomplices to cruelty.

The cost of looking away is not only measured in lives lost. It is measured in the death of our own conscience. Each silence erodes our humanity. Each indifference builds a world where cruelty thrives unchecked.

But this book is not only about leaders. It is about us. Every citizen who looked away, every person who excused indifference, became part of the machinery that sustains atrocity. The human cost is measured not only in Gaza's dead but in the death of our collective conscience.

There is still a choice. The cycle of indifference can be broken. Compassion can be reclaimed. "Never again" can be restored to its true meaning. But only if we move from witness to action. Only if we speak, resist, and demand justice, even when it costs us comfort.

We are all witnesses. History has already written that part. What remains unwritten is whether we were also accomplices.

The choice is ours. To witness with action, or to betray humanity once more. But cycles can be broken. Compassion can be reclaimed. And history, though heavy, is not immovable. The choice is before us now, as it has always been: to witness and act, or to look away and betray our humanity again.

The truth is this, to cherish the memories of those who perished under Hitler's genocide of the Jews is to sincerely and truly say "never again" to those who are committing this genocide against the Palestinian Arabs, Christians and Muslims alike.

GENEVA – Israel has committed genocide against Palestinians in the Gaza Strip, the UN Independent International Commission of Inquiry on the Occupied Palestinian Territory, claimed.

The UN Independent International Commission September 16, 2025

Courtesy of: Source Ohchr.org

GENEVA – "Israel has committed genocide against Palestinians in the Gaza Strip, the UN Independent International Commission of Inquiry on the Occupied Palestinian Territory, including East Jerusalem, and Israel said in a new report today. The Commission urges Israel and all States to fulfil their legal obligations under international law to end the genocide and punish those responsible for it.

The Commission has been investigating the events on and since 7 October 2023 for the last two years, and concluded that Israeli authorities and Israeli security forces committed four of the five genocidal acts defined by the 1948 Convention on the Prevention and Punishment of the Crime of Genocide, namely killing, causing serious bodily or mental harm, deliberately inflicting conditions of life calculated to bring about the destruction of the Palestinians in whole or in part, and imposing measures intended to prevent births.

Explicit statements by Israeli civilian and military authorities and the pattern of conduct of the Israeli security forces indicate that the genocidal acts were committed with intent to destroy, in whole or in part, Palestinians in the Gaza Strip as a group.

"The Commission finds that Israel is responsible for the commission of genocide in Gaza," said Navi Pillay, Chair of the Commission. "It is clear that there is an intent to destroy the Palestinians in Gaza through acts that meet the criteria set forth in the Genocide Convention."

"The responsibility for these atrocity crimes lies with Israeli authorities at the highest echelons who have orchestrated a genocidal campaign for almost two years now with the specific intent to destroy the Palestinian group in Gaza," Pillay said. "The Commission also finds that Israel has failed to prevent and punish the commission of genocide, through failure to investigate genocidal acts and to prosecute alleged perpetrators."

The report is based on all the Commission's prior investigations, as well as factual and legal findings in relation to attacks in Gaza carried out by Israeli forces, and the conduct and statements of Israeli authorities from 7 October 2023 until 31 July 2025.

The Commission's findings are based on a comprehensive examination of the underlying acts of genocide (actus reus) and genocidal intent (dolus specialis).

In establishing the genocidal acts, the Commission examined the Israeli military operations in Gaza, including killing and seriously harming unprecedented numbers of Palestinians; imposing a total siege, including blocking humanitarian aid leading to starvation; systematically destroying the healthcare and education systems in Gaza; committing systematic acts of sexual and gender based violence; directly targeting children; carrying out systematic and widespread attacks on religious and cultural sites; and disregarding the orders of the International Court of Justice.

In establishing genocidal intent, the Commission applied the "only reasonable inference" standard set forth by the International Court of Justice in the case of Bosnia v. Serbia. The Commission analysed statements made by Israeli authorities and concluded that those statements are direct evidence of genocidal intent. The Commission also analysed the pattern of conduct of Israeli authorities and the Israeli security forces in Gaza, including imposing starvation and inhumane conditions of life for Palestinians in Gaza, and found that genocidal intent was the only reasonable inference that could be concluded from the nature of their operations.

"Israel has flagrantly disregarded the orders for provisional measures from the International Court of Justice and warnings from Member States, UN offices, human rights organisations and civil society groups, and continued the strategy of destruction of the Palestinians in Gaza," said Pillay. "The Commission finds that the Israeli authorities had no intention to change their course of actions. On the contrary, Israeli authorities have persisted and continued with their genocidal campaign in Gaza for almost two years now. Israel must immediately end the genocide in Gaza and comply fully with the orders for provisional measures of the International Court of Justice," she added.

The acts of Israeli political and military leaders are attributable to the State of Israel. The Commission therefore concluded that the State of Israel bears responsibility for the failure to prevent genocide, the commission of genocide and the failure to punish the perpetrators of genocide against the Palestinians in the Gaza Strip.

The Commission also concluded that Israeli President Isaac Herzog, Prime Minister Benjamin Netanyahu and then Defense Minister Yoav Gallant, have incited the commission of genocide and that Israeli authorities have failed to take action against them to punish this incitement. The Commission has not fully assessed statements by other Israeli political and military leaders and considers that they too should be assessed to determine whether they constitute incitement to commit genocide.

The Commission urges the Government of Israel to comply immediately with its international legal obligations, including to end the genocide in the Gaza Strip and fully implement the provisional measures orders of the International Court of Justice.

Israel must end its policy of starvation, lift the siege and facilitate and ensure the unimpeded access of humanitarian aid at scale and unhindered access of all United Nations staff, including UNRWA and OHCHR international staff, and all recognized international humanitarian agencies delivering and coordinating aid. The Commission calls on Israel to immediately end the activities of the Gaza Humanitarian Foundation.

The Commission recommended that Member States cease the transfer of arms and other equipment that may be used for the commission of genocidal acts to Israel; ensure individuals and corporations in their territories and within their jurisdiction are not involved in aiding and assisting the commission of genocide or incitement to commit genocide; and take action on accountability through investigations and legal proceedings against individuals or corporations that are involved in the genocide directly or indirectly.

"The international community cannot stay silent on the genocidal campaign launched by Israel against the Palestinian people in Gaza. When clear signs and evidence of genocide emerge, the absence of action to stop it amounts to complicity," said Pillay. "Every day of inaction costs lives and erodes the credibility of the international community. All States are under a legal obligation to use all means that are reasonably available to them to stop the genocide in Gaza,"" she added. ENDS

Access to the UN full report here

https://www.ohchr.org/sites/default/files/documents/hrbodies/hrcouncil/sessions-

regular/session60/advance-version/a-hrc-60-
crp-3.pdf

Background:

The UN Independent International Commission
of Inquiry on the Occupied Palestinian
Territory, including East Jerusalem, and
Israel was established by the UN Human Rights
Council on 27 May 2021 to "investigate, in the
Occupied Palestinian Territory, including East
Jerusalem, and in Israel, all alleged violations of
international humanitarian law and all alleged
violations and abuses of international human rights
law leading up to and since 13 April
2021." Resolution A/HRC/RES/S-30/1 further
requested the commission of inquiry to "investigate
all underlying root causes of recurrent tensions,
instability and protraction of conflict, including
systematic discrimination and repression based on
national, ethnic, racial or religious identity."

For media queries, please contact: Todd Pitman,
Media Adviser for the UN Human Rights Council's
Investigative Bodies:

todd.pitman@un.org / +41766911761; or

Pascal Sim, Human Rights Council Media Officer: simp@un.org.

References
Recommended Reading

Amnesty International. (2024, December 19). *Extermination and acts of genocide: Israel deliberately depriving Palestinians in Gaza.* Amnesty International. https://www.amnesty.org/en/latest/news/2024/12/amnesty-international-concludes-israel-is-committing-genocide-against-palestinians-in-gaza

Arendt, H. (1963). *Eichmann in Jerusalem: A report on the banality of evil.* Viking Press.

Bandura, A. (1999). Moral disengagement in the perpetration of inhumanities. *Personality and Social Psychology Review, 3*(3), 193–209. https://doi.org/10.1207/s15327957pspr0303_3

Human Rights Watch. (2025, February 7). *Gaza: Israel's unlawful attacks, mass civilian deaths.* Human Rights Watch. https://www.hrw.org/news/2025/02/07/gaza-israels-unlawful-attacks-mass-civilian-deaths

Independent International Commission of Inquiry on the Occupied Palestinian Territory, including East Jerusalem, and Israel. (2025, September 16). *Legal analysis of the conduct of Israel in Gaza pursuant to the Convention on the Prevention and Punishment of the Crime of Genocide* (A/HRC/60/CRP.3). United Nations

Human Rights Council.
https://www.ohchr.org/sites/default/files/documents/hrb
odies/hrcouncil/sessions-regular/session60/advance-
version/a-hrc-60-crp-3.pdf

Independent International Commission of Inquiry on
the Occupied Palestinian Territory, including East
Jerusalem, and Israel. (2025, June 12). *Report of the
Independent International Commission of Inquiry on the
Occupied Palestinian Territory, including East Jerusalem,
and Israel* (A/HRC/59/26). United Nations Human
Rights Council.
https://www.un.org/unispal/document/report-of-the-
independent-international-commission-of-inquiry-on-
the-occupied-palestinian-territory-including-east-
jerusalem-and-israel-a-hrc-59-26/

Khoureis, A. (2025). *The compassionate leadership model
and pyramid: Ascending empathy: Unveiling the seven-level
path and journey of compassionate leadership.* ANG Power
Publishing House, Los Angeles, CA.

Médecins Sans Frontières. (2025, March 18). *MSF
condemns Israel's continuous attacks on hospitals and
medical staff in Gaza.* Médecins Sans Frontières.
https://www.msf.org/msf-condemns-israels-continuous-
attacks-hospitals-and-medical-staff-gaza

Milgram, S. (1974). *Obedience to authority.* Harper &
Row.

United Nations Office of the High Commissioner for Human Rights. (2025, September 16). *Israel has committed genocide in the Gaza Strip, UN commission finds* [Press release]. United Nations. https://www.ohchr.org/en/press-releases/2025/09/israel-has-committed-genocide-gaza-strip-un-commission-finds

United Nations. (1948, December 9). *Convention on the Prevention and Punishment of the Crime of Genocide.* United Nations Treaty Series, 78, 277. https://www.un.org/en/genocideprevention/genocide-convention.shtml

United Nations. (1945, August 8). *Charter of the International Military Tribunal (Nuremberg Charter).* United Nations. https://www.un.org/en/genocideprevention/documents/atrocity-crimes/Doc.2_Charter%20of%20IMT%202945.pdf

United Nations Human Rights Council. (2025, September 16). *Legal analysis of the conduct of Israel in Gaza pursuant to the Convention on the Prevention and Punishment of the Crime of Genocide* (A/HRC/60/CRP.3). Office of the High Commissioner for Human Rights. https://www.ohchr.org/sites/default/files/documents/hrbodies/hrcouncil/sessions-regular/session60/advance-version/a-hrc-60-crp-3.pdf

United Nations Human Rights Council. (1999, June 7). *Report of the independent inquiry into the actions of the United Nations during the 1994 genocide in Rwanda* (S/1999/1257). United Nations. https://undocs.org/S/1999/1257

About Dr. Abraham Khoureis, Ph.D.

Dr. Abraham Khoureis, Ph.D., is a multi-talented thought leader and partner, author, an award-winning mentor, and advocate for compassionate leadership. He is an adjunct professor who specializes in teaching graduate-level courses in business and management, blending academic theory with real-world business practices. Dr. Khoureis is also a small business owner and holds numerous state certifications and professional designations and licenses, highlighting his multidisciplinary expertise.

He is the creator of the Compassionate Leadership Model and Pyramid, which emphasizes leadership built on self-awareness, mindfulness, and commitment to serving others without expectation of return. This seven-level model pyramid, with "Community" as its fifth level, reflects his vision of leadership that positively impacts the broader community and society.

Moreover, Dr. Khoureis developed the Disability Learning Attainment Model, a framework designed to empower individuals with disabilities through inclusive education, skill-building, and leadership development. His work champions and empowers inclusivity, accessibility, and ethical practices in both education and leadership. He has been published on *Forbes.com*,

Newsweek.com, and the distinguished *Leader to Leader Journal*. He was recognized as LinkedIn's Top Leadership and Management Voice, and Thinkers360's Top 50 Voices.

Dr. Abraham's contributions extend to his writings, professional development initiatives, and thought leadership, making him a respected emerging leader in the fields of compassionate leadership, organizational behavior, and human resources development.

Easily accessible at:
DrAbeKhoureis.com – DrAbeBooks.com

Social Media: @DrAbeKhoureis

On Amazon.com, search for Dr. Abraham Khoureis

Other Books by Dr. Abraham Khoureis, Ph.D.

The Balance In Between: Finding the Balance Between Emotional Intelligence and Emotional Stupidity. ISBN: 979-8-9895211-2-8

Hollywood Dream: How To Make It In Tinseltown ISBN: 979-8-9895211-7-3

Decoding Microaggressions for Leaders and Beyond: Understanding Microaggressions Face-to-Face. ISBN: 979-8-9895211-4-2

Reasonable Accommodation: Empowering Inclusion. ISBN: 979-8-9895211-3-5

SELF: Introducing The Self Rotating Model. ISBN: 979-8-9895211-5-9

The Compassionate Leadership Model and Pyramid. ISBN: 979-8-9895211-0-4

Revealing The Seven Secrets to Exceptional Mentorship. ISBN: 979-8-9895211-8-0

For his latest published books:

Visit Amazon.com, search for Dr. Abraham Khoureis

www.ingramcontent.com/pod-product-compliance
Lightning Source LLC
Chambersburg PA
CBHW031525040426
42445CB00009B/401